A Life Wasted…46 Minutes at a Time

(and other great things about television!)

Lori S. Gee

Copyright © 2012 by Lori S. Gee

All rights reserved.

No part of this book may be reproduced or transmitted in any form or by any means, electronic or mechanical, including photocopying, recording, or by any informational storage and retrieval system, without permission in writing from the publisher, except for the inclusion of brief quotations in a review.

Big Dream Media Creations

Big Dream Media Creations
P.O. Box 395
Eastlake, CO 80641-0395

www.bdmcinc.com

Published in the United States of America

2012

ISBN: 978-0-6156003-9-0

www.alifewastedbooks.com

FOR MARK

THANK YOU

CONTENTS

Acknowledgments	i.
Electronic Downfall	1
Tele-Piphany	9
Commercials and You. Why God Blessed Us with the DVR	14
News Programs (and other filler)	20
Soaps (and other beautiful people)	24
Sitcoms and Logic. Can they Co-exist?	28
This Old House. Don't Try This at Home!	33
Springers…You Know Who You Are	39
Reality Shows (are they really alien messages?)	43
Game Shows. I'll take the 'NEW CAR' Bob!!	47
Nature Shows. See Thumper, See Tigger, See Tigger Eat	53
Real Housewives (and other snotty bitches)	58
The Doctors. Curing *Your* Disease, Riiiiight After the Break!	64
Infomercials and You. Yes, You Really *Can* Change the Channel!	68
Auctions and You. Do You REALLY Have a Big Enough Garage?	76
Antique Roadshow. No Billy Bob, that Black Velvet Matador is *Not* an Early Van Gough	83
House Hunters. That's *How* Much?	89
Late Night (and other noise to have sex to)	95
Epilogue	98

ACKNOWLEDGMENTS

Thanks to my wonderful sister, Gail Lindsey, and also to my great friend, Olivia Coleman, for all of your help and encouragement!

Thanks also to our great friends in TV Land, for giving me something to write about!

Electronic Downfall

Like a lot of people, I've always liked to entertain grand fantasies and daydreams about my very soon to be exciting and glamorous life!

In my case, being a heterosexual female, I'd imagine sailing the high seas while travelling the world with Johnny Depp (of course hitting all the super-exotic ports, for my bikini photo shoots with Vogue magazine), while also writing a hit Broadway play (of course starring Johnny), then, the following week, I'd invent the next I-Pad!

I'd fight world hunger, world obesity, and socialism too, all while raising my 6 adopted children (because we don't want a stomach pooch after all), with my movie star hotty, along with his Oscar winning sideburns and ultra-hip beard.

Of course it also goes without saying that Johnny and I would be diligently working, along with the President and Secretary of State, to get rid of all those terrible land-mines, in that country whose name I can't spell or pronounce.

Yup, all of this, while still cooking up nine course 5-star dinners, and making quilts out of plastic trash bags for the homeless, in my spare time.

But, let's be real. Things happen, time goes by, yada, yada, yada, and, well, long story short, what I now have, instead of Johnny, is Hubby, a bona-fide Johnny look-a-like, if Johnny were to gain a lot of weight and lose a lot of hair. Hubby's been very busy and stressed lately, because he's in charge of planning our 25th anniversary dinner, at the local I.H.O.P.

Instead of a luxury yacht I have a 1985 mini-van that smells like stale burgers, and any photo shoots that I ever do have, usually involve those machines that cost a buck. With gas prices the way they are I guess the yacht was really a moot point, anyway.

The only charitable cause that I'm working on is the 'Women against Thinning Hair' organization, because I hope that, one day very soon, they'll be able to help me.

Looking back, now, I can see almost to the day, pretty much exactly when things started to head downhill.

It had been a pretty average day, overall, unless you'd considered the fact that I'd apparently contracted MALARIA or something even worse, and was feeling sicker than *any* human has ever been in the history of mankind! I swear to God, it felt like the Devil himself was standing on my chest and doing a rhumba.

Since I needed help Hubby of course was nowhere to be found. So, I stumbled shakily to the medicine cabinet to find that the only thing even vaguely resembling modern medicine, (from this century anyway), is a bottle of NyQuil that has been around so long it's actually gelled into a vile green gooey mess. Didn't matter, I was desperate.

I watered it down and proceeded to lay into that green slime like a camel that's finally been led to water after crossing the Gobi Desert during a drought. And, I had to say, it did help. The rhumba was now down to more of a slow waltz.

Around dinnertime or so (and another half bottle) I was feeling a bit, um, let's say nappy, and probably therefore a bit more agreeable than usual. At least when I'm conscious, that is.

Hubby, being very concerned for my wellbeing (also knowing I'll probably be out cold for hours) decided to take this agreeable opportunity (and, for some reason, our largest credit card), to promptly drive to the nearest Mini-Mega-Mall, where he very thoughtfully proceeded to buy a bottle of Advil, knowing that he'll probably have a headache whenever I wake up.

With that accomplished (and since he had the credit card), he'd then decided to just 'browse around' a bit. Maybe he'd finally buy that new garden hoe he knew I'd had my eye on, or something useful like that. After all he's always just thinking about what's best for his family!

Somehow, though, during his valiant search for the garden section (of the Best Buy Electronics store), he'd instead "mistakenly" ended up in the TV Aisle (which apparently isn't required to have a marked exit), where he became a bit "lost, dizzy and disoriented!".

"What a crazy thing it was! I wasn't anywhere near the TV section!" he'd later explain, "I *know* that we really need new garden equipment, not a new TV! You know that I only want what's best for the family!"

Recalling the event afterward, the only thing he knows for sure is that he was trying his "*very* darndest" to find a salesman, to show him to the latest in the new designer hoes, when "somehow, something in his head just sort of snapped" and he was suddenly in the middle of what could only be described as a "crazy seizure or something", during which he "lost track of all time and knowledge" (but, miraculously, not the credit card).

It was while he was under this *severe* impairment, (what, nobody could call 911?) that he'd "innocently and unknowingly" managed to make "just a *minor* purchase". It just wasn't his fault, you see. It was totally out of his control.

Hmmm, *quite* a story.

As it turns out, this *minor* purchase is also what's known as the Very Latest (and most expensive) High Tech Flat-screen LCD HDTV 1080P, featuring GSA 4400 Television Technology!! (Oooooh, ahhhhh!) Including at least 95 different features, most of which I don't know what they are (I don't really think that Hubby does, either).

"We all know how these things can happen, to even the best of us", he pleaded later, while trying to appear properly sheepish and regretful. Especially considering that he looked perfectly healthy at the time. (Well, as healthy as he ever does, anyway.)

"I've heard on the news that these new 3-D TV's are causing *exactly* these types of reactions, all across the country!!" he says. "Someone should look into this! We were lucky! It could have been *so* much worse!!"

Soon afterward, when he'd "finally come around to his senses, and was feeling much better, 'thank God!'" he'd realized his devastating mistake. He knew, after all, that we have a perfectly good TV already, and that what we *really* needed was new garden equipment, not the latest in entertainment and video gaming! He never would have done this in his right mind!

The problem now was what to *do* with this gleaming and beautiful (and totally unnecessary) new entertainment system? It was on clearance, and so, understandably, non-refundable. What a waste of money. He felt terrible!

But the worst part was that, with our appallingly outdated and obsolete (i.e., last year's model) sound system, the new TV and gaming system were barely even usable! Let alone state of the art! Gosh, what *had* he done?!

After careful consideration of the various options, (along with a quick call to Visa to check the remaining available credit) he'd decided that there simply was no other answer that made any sense.

He might as well just go ahead and "fix the problem" by also purchasing the obligatory overpriced and overpowered sound system, with its 'Larger Than Life 1550DB SOUND AT 20W!', and 'Very High GB MHZ' something or other, that's apparently going to "CHANGE THE WAY WE WATCH TELEVISION!". You know, since the damage was *already* done and all.

At least we'd be getting the "best value" for our now lost savings, he mentioned afterward, quite proud of how much money he was, at least in his mind anyway, *saving* us.

By the time I came to, the next morning, it was already too late. My only choice at this point was simply to accept it, take an Advil and more NyQuil, and just agree to the full complement of cable, including over 400 channels of news, sports, and daytime talk TV (that's just in Spanish alone!), simply because I was just too sick to say no.

Once we added the DVR and Blue-Ray to the package, my destiny was set firmly in place.

It became apparent, very quickly, that all hope was lost.

There'd be *no* intelligent and sparkling dinner conversations at the White House, with the President and Secretary of State.

There'd be *no* climbing 14'ers, while raising money for the Blind Athletes against Breast Cancer. And, unfortunately, those awful land-mines will remain right where they are.

No, there'd not even be a badly needed pedicure, simply because my nail tech can only fit me in during the 'Wheel of Fortune!', which just won't do!

Nope, when it comes right down to it I need to be at home, to make sure the DVR always has room for the next great show!

I should also admit that, at this point anyway, I really have absolutely *no* idea if this book will ever be finished, or not. It's not that I don't have the time or the motivation, and I even have (what I think, anyway) are a few good ideas to share (not to mention a word processor that includes a spell-checker and word-count).

No, it's really more a matter of whether or not the creative folks of TV land will actually *allow* me to take the hour (or so) that I plan this book will take (or, in TV terms, around 46 minutes (not counting commercials).

Suffice it to say, if you're reading this now, you can safely assume that either, a: our TV cable has been destroyed by a gang of anti-TV terrorists, or, b: I forgot to pay the cable bill, which I swore that I would, right after the "Price is

Right" marathon on TBS. (I just love how Bob Barker still looks *exactly* like he did in 1973!)

It's just plain out of my hands.

Tele-Piphany!

It hasn't always been this way for me. Like most red-blooded Americans, I grew up with TV, and have certainly watched my share over the years (I can sing along with 9 out of 10 commercial jingles, and 39 out of 43 theme songs, from, oh, let's say, the last 40,(or so) years.) So I was, quite obviously, a fan.

But, also like most red-blooded Americans, I've had to earn a living, by working at a JOB.

The JOB, along with sleeping, commuting, family time, sex, and volunteering for the 'Homeless Hippy's Against Balding Project', was quite time consuming, and really left only a few short hours, per day, to catch up with America's favorite programs.

So you see, it just wasn't possible to be a true TV junkie during those years, there simply wasn't enough time in the day.

That all changed, though, last year, when I was fired, um, I mean downsized (I prefer retired) from above said JOB, which, believe it or not, I was secretly thrilled about!

Now I'd finally be able to seriously focus on my *real* life's passions (including Johnny and the landmines), as well as catching up on the backlog of sock darning, grout cleaning, and detailing the cat! This is going to be great!

And it was…for a while.

But it didn't take very long at all, though, before I realized that even the most demanding darning, cleaning and cat detail jobs took surprisingly less time than I'd ever thought they would (I also learned that cats *really* don't like vacuum cleaners, but that's another chapter).

It also quickly became clear that the exotic world travel and yachts I'd dreamed of, not to mention hob-knobbing with Heads of State and Movie Stars, would require not only a bit more energy and time than I really wanted to expend, but, more importantly, just a bit more money than I'd anticipated.

Needless to say this presented a bit of a problem with Hubby, who's not only afraid of water and yachts to begin with, but also doesn't give a crap how dirty the cat is, or if the socks *ever* get darned. Plus Johnny wouldn't return any of my calls.

I was mulling this challenge one day, shortly after our (Hubby's) new TV had arrived, while at the same time catching up on the latest episode of "Los Ricos Tambie'n Llor (The Rich Also Cry), "An exotic and moving show, about a homeless woman who's been adopted by a rich man. She has men falling love with her, throughout the drama, but she's still true to her savior!", when I swear to you that God actually came down from Heaven and spoke *directly* to me, and *finally* gave me my answer!

I could simply live vicariously through the stars and wannabe's in TV-Land, instead. And, in doing so, I'd save *all* of that energy, time, and money (especially money)!

This, I reasoned, was the 'best for the family', especially since we were down to just one income, and all. Also now that most of our savings were gone, too.

As a wonderful bonus I'd never have to leave the sofa, and nobody would care if I wear my jammies for a solid 3 days in a row without washing them, because I'm still deciding which laundry soap I should be loyal to.

Best yet! The more that I watch, the more energy, time, and money (especially money) I save! Again, for the good of the family!

This finally made perfect sense! Hallelujah!! (Insert chorus of angels here.) Why didn't I think of it before!

Not only could I live out my lifelong fantasies and dreams, while resting my neck on the microwaveable beanie pillow, I also knew that when Johnny finally *did* call, we'd have many deep and sincere conversations about the latest B-Listers on Dancing with the Stars, not to mention the new Brady Bunch Reunion four part mini-series.

Now I was getting excited. It was time to move past the TV hobbyist that I'd always been! Now I could *always* keep up with the Kardashians, all 20 showings of them a day, (maybe it just seems like that many), with no JOB or DREAMS to come between us!

We could forge a strong and lasting relationship, together! Plus the non-stop censor beeping and terrible grammar (not to mention the beer and inertia) would also help to kill off some of those pesky brain cells that keep telling me, "I should really find a new job".

Now, you may be asking yourself, why would she possibly be willing to lose that precious, and valuable TV time, (around 46 minutes or so), to write this book?

Well, trust me, there are many complex, and very interesting reasons, but mostly it boils down to one main point. Even when you're retired, (um, between jobs), you must remember that you still have important bills to pay!

At the top of the list there's the cable bill, along with the monthly installment payments for the TV's (4 out of 7 of them anyway). There's also the electricity for the TV's, and the batteries for the TV remotes, not to mention the anti-static wipes for the screens.

And don't even get me started about the latest 'co-ax titanium high velocity 1200 cables' that Hubby says we need to buy, because, otherwise, "we might as well be watching a 10inch black and white, without foil for the rabbit ears!" (Brother, what a drama queen!)

So anyway, with that in mind, along with the fact that Hubby's not yet exactly, (ahem), shall we say, *aware* of my 'retirement', I must therefore console him with the fact that my TV time is indeed valuable research for this project, and will also someday be used to stop global warming and save the planet! (Also, that I may possibly increase this year's earnings enough to actually be required to file a federal income tax return).

Of course you and I both know that the insight to be gained from my experience is invaluable, regardless of who makes the money (and who doesn't), but I don't really mention that to Hubby. In the meantime I just thank God he still has a *real* job, so that I can continue on with my research!

Assuming the power doesn't fail, that is.

Commercials and You. Why God Blessed us with DVR's

Today's To-Do

- Groceries (buy Prep H) – check
- Laundry (4 loads) - check
- Feed & Water Dog - check
- Clean up Puddle of Dog Puke - check
- Kitchen Knob Cleaning and Disinfection - check
- Dog Walk and Poo Patrol – check
- Write Chapter for Best Selling Book - check
- Nap – check

It's 7:25a.m. Time for some commercials!

As the old joke goes, DVR's are God's way of showing that he loves us, and wants us to be happy!

Ok, I think it may have really been started about beer, originally, but, as an accomplished expert in both subjects, I can honestly say that comparing the two would be like comparing having only one Johnny Depp, when you could have five or six instead.

Why would you possibly want just one, when you could have some studly extras around to do the menial chores for you, such as the weekly shopping and Porche waxing, while also hand building a new boathouse for the luxury yacht?

Who cares then, when the original spends his days on the couch in his underwear, playing War craft 889? I will, in fact, strongly encourage *all* of my Johnny's to spend the day in his underwear (not to mention mine).

Sorry, I digress. I tend to do when he comes to mind, especially if he's half-dressed.

Anyway, back to the DVR. This, in my opinion anyway, is quite nearly the greatest invention ever! It's just behind electricity, cable, and Johnny.

No, wait. Make that electricity, Johnny, and *then* cable. (Electricity only comes first, because, without that he wouldn't have a way to call me; at 303-611-1750 (mornings are best). Sorry, wandering again.

Before we got our DVR, and could seamlessly skip and ignore the commercials, our lives were simply exhausting!

Filled with youthful exuberance, childless-ness, and nonstop commercial breaks, Hubby and I'd always felt compelled to get out in the world. Experience the good life!

We'd see the new movies and eat at the very best (most expensive anyway) restaurants. We'd attend the latest Broadway plays (just like the ones I'd write soon), and we'd buy the latest in oversize luxury cars that would make us taller, smarter, and more popular! We really did do it all!

What eventually happened, though, is both ironic and odd, but, mostly, just kind of sad.

With all the dinners and fun we were having soon we had less and less TV time, not to mention less money (way less money). So, as it went, the more fun that we'd have, the fewer commercials we'd see. The fewer commercials we'd see, the less fun that we'd have.

It wasn't that we didn't *want* to have fun anymore, we just simply no longer *knew* about the new movies with the Oscar nomination buzz. Or the best restaurants, that served the finest in free-range Buffalo meat.

Or even the newest sports car that would grow Hubby's hair back, and give him washboard abs while getting an astounding 120mpg in the city! (We'd already agreed that Broadway plays were pretty much like having your fingernails forcibly removed, so that was mostly a non-issue.)

Somehow, by the end of it all, we'd ended up with absolutely nothing better to do (and no money to do it anyway), except, yup, you guessed it. Watch TV!

I know!! Right!? It's the chicken and the egg thing, all over again!

Anyway, it was just around this time that we learned of a new gadget that just became available, called the DVR, which, I now like to think of, as the DEVINE RECORDER (insert chorus of angels here). "Take control over your TV and your life!" the ad said. Of course we just had to have it!

After the long weeks of expecting (and choosing names), we finally delivered our DVR, (oops, I mean the cable company delivered her (insert another chorus of angels here)), and we couldn't have been prouder!

We were like any new parents, not exactly sure how to handle her, always afraid that we might drop her! But, we learned quickly, and soon became bonded, as a *family*. In fact she became more than a member of the family; she's actually become a *part* of us.

We named her Avatar (*Hinduism* - a god's coming in bodily form to earth), for reasons that I think are fairly obvious. Hubby went along with it because he liked the naked blue chick in the movie.

Avatar always knows what shows we love. When they're on, and what channel, too. And she *always* makes sure, that we have the very latest programming options to select from.

She also gives us *invaluable* advice, not only about which programs we might like best, but, even more importantly, which ones we wouldn't!

And she's proven to be a loving and caring companion as well, by always looking out for our best interests! She somehow knew from the beginning that it would save us enormous amounts of energy, time, and money, by never again forcing us to view those nasty, tempting commercials, and she makes it her priority that we don't have to ever face that kind of pressure.

I just don't know what we ever did without her!

Lately there's been some, ahem, 'talk' in the household, that "maybe we can't really *afford* her anymore", (now that I don't have a JOB), and that "maybe she should be taken to the local shelter" (cable company), "where they can look after her properly" (rent her to some scumbag, that won't dust her properly). I suggested that perhaps Hubby should be the one sent to the shelter...

Once I'd bailed Hubby out of the shelter (okay, I really just paid his bar tab, at the local pub), we had a deep and honest (drunken) discussion about our finances, and we both were in agreement. It was really much cheaper to keep our dear Avatar, than to continually pay for his beer tab.

Anyway, back to the commercials. As you've probably guessed by now, it's actually been quite a while since I'd been 'commercia-ssaulted', thanks to our little Avatar! She's such a good and diligent girl that I actually had to shut her off for a time (we prefer to say nappy-time), just to be able to view a few ads, to write this chapter.

I'm pretty sure that she knows, but she's playing it cool.

I feel so cheap, and dirty.

News programs (and other filler)

Today's To-Do

- Car Wash 2 cars (automatic, of course) – check
- Oil Change 2 cars (also automatic) – check
- Feed & Water the Cat – check
- Cleanup Puddle of Cat Puke - check
- Litter-box Cleaning and Disinfection - check
- Another Dog Walk and Poo Patrol – check
- Write Next Chapter for Best Selling Book - check
- Nap – check

It's 9:00a.m. Time for the news!

"This just in to the News-Now Newsroom!!" *(This week's intern, whose name we can't pronounce, e-mailed us a link that he found on his Mom's Facebook page)*

"We've got breaking news!!" *(We were planning to tell you this story anyway, after the break, but hey, we've got some extra time to fill right now)*

"Man eaten by Duckbilled Platypus, next on Eye Witness News!!" *(We're going to make you sit thru at least 6 more commercial breaks, before we **finally** tell the story of an adorable*

Platypus named Sweetie, who was fed gingerbread men, as a special holiday treat at the zoo)

"Lisa's here next, to give us our pinpoint forecast! She'll give an hour by hour forecast, so you'll know *exactly* what weather, *and when*, to expect in your neighborhood"*(Give us a break, they can't even do that at the equator)*

Alright, before you get the wrong idea, I really do have the greatest respect for our hard working men and women in the media. After all, without them how else would we know about the latest miracle drug that's going to help us lose 80% of our body weight, while raising our I.Q. and increasing our car's gas mileage twenty percent. All *without* giving up Twinkies?

Or, the 'Important Safety Tips for Driving in a Snowstorm!' (Watch for icy roads and for *gosh sake's* slow down!).

But my opinion is, quite simply, that these shows just have *way* too much time to fill, when, (if you get right down to it), the reality is that it's a pretty dull world some days (we call those weekdays), and there just isn't that much to report. Especially if it happens to be a slow weather day, to boot.

Just how *do* you keep people informed and entertained, for about 46 minutes, when there's just plain nothing to say? (Hmm. I'd better figure that out right quick.)

Anyway, our local news-teams here in my hometown are legendary pros at creatively filling their time gaps with less than newsy items (yeah, Channel 7 I'm talking about you).

They promote their patented '10 Minutes of Non-Stop News!' at least 5 times an hour, but what they fail to mention is that it's actually for the whole frigging 46 minutes they'll be on the air! Yikes!

They employ such techniques, as: 'The Weather Crawl' - During the forecast put up a statewide weather map, while the *'Chief Meteorologist!'* reads ALL 35 freakin' cities, along with EACH and EVERY of their respective expected temperatures for the next 3 days! Man, talk about mindlessly increasing your word-count!

(Speaking of that, according to my nifty, shnifty word-count function, I see that I'm now at 2,474 words. Hmm… Just how many words does it take, to make a book anyway? Am I almost done?)

(Crap! I just looked up the average word-count of a standard 200 page paperback, and it's somewhere around 50,000 words! I'm beginning to think I may not make my estimated 46 minutes.)

Other filler tactics include: 'The Time Killer' – Cute and adorable back and forth banter among the anchors, so we all know that they're one big happy family! Yeah, right. If they spend their miserable, tension-filled Thanksgivings at

Aunt Bessie's, arguing over who makes the best black eyed pea stuffing while the dog eats the turkey off the table in the kitchen, and Uncle Ed's passed out in the recliner from too much sparkling cider, *that* counts as *family*!

And finally, my personal favorite: 'The Strip Tease' – Pause at least eight times during the 5 o'clock news to tell us what they're working on, for 10 o'clock. Isn't that like me telling you at 5 o'clock, that I'll be writing this book from 10:00 to 10:46? Who cares? Until 10:46?

The odd contradiction on the news programs, though, is that with all the time that they need to fill, why do they bother to invite studio guests for an interview, when the very first question posed to the guest about their particular topic, is followed with "very quickly, we've only got 7 seconds left!"? And yet they'll spend 14 minutes beforehand, promoting that same interview!?

And what the heck is up with these cable news shows, lately, where the anchors do nothing but sit and surf the net, then read us the headlines? Can't I just sit in my jammies and do the same thing on a COMPUTER? Without the annoying anchormen, and their spray-on hair?

But again, as I said before, I do admire and revere these folks, because without them where else would be get our important day's news? I mean besides newspapers, the internet, telephone, magazines, books, radio, government publications, leaflets, flyers, ham radio, carrier pigeons, and the good old rumor mill?

Soaps (and other beautiful people)

Today's To-Do

- Dental Appointment (request the gas) – check
- Post Office – check (I think)
- Dog Wash & Trim Nails – check
- Apply Bandages to Dog Bites and Scratches - check
- Light-bulb Cleaning and Disinfection - check
- Another Dog Walk and Poo Patrol – check
- Write Next Chapter for Best Selling Book - check
- Nap – check

It's 10:30a.m. Time for the soaps!

Fade In:

Interior Bedroom – Morning

The bedroom (recently featured in both Better Homes and Gardens *and* House Beautiful in the same month) is bathed in a golden soft light (almost heavenly, you could say) where we see the attractive couple lounging on their California king featherbed, with 18000 count sheets and 28000 count comforter, reading the morning paper while enjoying their imported tea, drinking from the antique platinum teapot (formerly used by Queen Elizabeth) along with the delicious imported crumpets, that came from that country with all the landmines.

JOHNNY is dapper in his Ralph Lauren smoking jacket and silk pajamas, and his eyes are shining, exactly the same Azure of the untamed ocean outside!

LORI is ravishing in her De La Renta gown and Manolo Blahnik heeled slippers. (In the morning light, she looks at least 20 years younger than her age, looking 'uncannily' like a younger Angelina Jolie.)

She glances towards the ocean, and is again so very thankful they were able to *finally* call this place home! After all they'd been through!

She'd have been so very happy with just the 20,000 square feet Tudor and the prime 20 acres of beachfront property with its' beautiful endangered exotic woods forest, which will be soon be used to build the new boathouse for the luxury yacht.

The 10 car garage, servant's quarters, and 3 guest houses were merely an extra blessing!

But again she thinks of the accident, and her Emerald Green eyes cloud with tears, somehow making her even *more* beautiful!

Johnny

(Slow piano music) We've got to put that all behind us now, we've got each other and that's *all* that matters. *You're* my life now!

Lori

(More slow piano music) But Johnny, what will become of those landmines? Those people still need us, and we just *can't* let them down!

Johnny

(More slow piano music) *God* you're beautiful!!! But you *know* that I'm the only surgeon that can perform that surgery. Nobody else can *save* him! You *know* that!

Lori

(More slow piano music) But Johnny, you *know* that he forced your Father into bankruptcy, and stole his wife (your own *mother!*) from you! Why *should* you save his life?!

Johnny

(Add a couple of sinister notes to the slow piano music) Let's just say it's because I have…(Cue the bahm bahm bahm !! sound) 'other' plans for him!

Fade out: (add a couple more sinister notes to the slow piano music) as they stare longingly into each other's incredible Azure and Emerald Green eyes.

Fade in:

Interior Bedroom – Morning

Although two months have elapsed (real-time), we again join Lori and Johnny, about 46 minutes later. Their eyes are *still* questioning, and Johnny, again, is overwhelmed by her intoxicating beauty!

He begins to rub her shoulder gently, feeling her tremble at his very touch. God, she's beautiful!

Just then the doorbell rings. Johnny goes to answer. His Azure eyes widen at the sight!

Johnny

(Sinister piano) Mother!

Mother

(More sinister piano) Johnny!

Fade out: (Keep playing. Sigh) Another stare down. Sigh.

Sitcoms and Logic. Can they Co-exist?

Today's To-Do

- Write Checks for Overdue Bills - check
- Mow Overgrown Lawn - check
- Cat Detail and Nail Trim - check
- Apply Bandages to Cat Bites and Scratches - check
- Phone Cleaning and Disinfection – check
- Another Dog Walk and Poo Patrol – check
- Write Next Chapter for Best Selling Book - check
- Nap – check

It's 11:00a.m. Time for some comedy!

Fade In:

Interior Bedroom – Morning

(Lead in with 5-8 notes of rock music)

The bedroom, recently featured in the last flopped sitcom series (cancelled after one episode) is bathed in a harsh, greenish light, ever since the studio execs have decided to save money by buying fluorescent lights, (almost ghoulish, you could say), where we see the couple lounging on their

Sealy Comfor-Pedic they bought in a thrift store shortly after they married, in 1984.

You can hear the rustling of the 40 count sheets and Wal-Mart comforter as they read the morning paper while enjoying their Sanka, served in a plastic pitcher they found in their neighbor's recycling bin (not that they *normally* go through the neighbor's trash, but it was an emergency) along with stale mini-powdered doughnuts, imported from the local Mini-Mart.

HUBBY (Johnny would NEVER sink as low as doing a sitcom!) looks drawn and tired, and a little pastier than usual, after his long night of drinking beer with his 'lovably loser' buddies.

LORI is ravishing in her De La Renta gown and Manolo Blahnik heeled slippers. (In the morning light, she looks at least 20 years younger than her age, looking 'uncannily' like a younger Angelina Jolie).

She glances towards the chain link dog run outside of the filthy window, and is again shocked at how she ended up here!

If she'd have married Johnny, when she'd had the chance, she'd be living in a 20,000 square feet Tudor, with the prime 20 acres of beachfront property and its' beautiful endangered exotic woods forest, which will soon be used to build the new boathouse for the luxury yacht!

The 10 car garage, servant's quarters, and 3 guest houses would have been merely a bonus.

Now, she'd just have to learn to be happy with a double-wide trailer, which pre-dates her first car, along with a depression-era kitchenette, and a falling down carport they share with their 'hilariously stereotypical' neighbors, in the trailer next door.

Hubby

You plannin' on doin' some laundry today? I've been wearing this underwear so long they're about ready to stand up by *themselves*! (Cue laugh track)

Lori

Well maybe you ought to think about standing up *with* them! God *knows* you could use the exercise! (Cue laugh track)

Hubby

God you're beautiful!!! Anyway, this is just 'more of me to *love* baby!' (Cue laugh track)

Lori

Must be nice to live in your world doughboy! (Cue laugh track) Anyway, you know I have the Vogue photo shoot today! Maybe it's time you figured out what those 'big *scary* white boxes' are, that sit in our *laundry room,* you moron! (Cue laugh track)

Hubby

Yeah, well maybe you ought to figure out what that 'big box with burners' is, in the *kitchen*! Yeah! (Cue laugh track)

Lori

Yeah, well, I hadn't heard that Twinkies *needed* cooking, pasty-face! (Cue laugh track with excited applause)

Fade out: (add a couple more rock notes) He stares longingly into her Emerald Green eyes, while she stares back, annoyed, into his yellowish, watery ones.

Fade in:

Interior Laundry Room – Afternoon

(Lead in with 5-8 notes of rock music)

We see Hubby looking adorably muddled and confused, as he helplessly scans each of the 3 buttons that might *possibly* start the washing machine.

After several seconds with no luck, all the while being 'comically' entertaining, he finally throws the box of detergent on the floor and runs out of the room.

Fade out: (Another 5-8 rock notes. Sigh) Another commercial. Sigh

This Old House. Don't try this at home!

Today's To-Do

- Rake Leaves (throw into neighbor's yard) - check
- Dust Furniture (using Hubby's favorite 'Rock on Dude!' T-shirt) - check
- Trim Rosebushes (throw into neighbor's yard) - check
- Apply Bandages to Cuts and Scratches - check
- Another Dog Walk and Poo Patrol – check
- Write Next Chapter for Best Selling Book - check
- Nap – check

It's 12:00p.m. Time for Home Improvement!

(Drip, drip, drip) "Today, on Rachel Sue! We're going to tell the *heart-wrenching* story of a Korean Orphan, and her long pilgrimage to find her adoptive parents!" (Drip, drip, drip)

"This *very* brave young girl survived an ocean journey of over 2000 miles! *And*, get this! With *only* her Donald Duck inflatable water wings, keeping her afloat!" (Drip, drip, drip) [Cut to girl] "It was scary!"

(Drip, drip, drip) "Then, we're going to show you the *best* brownie recipe ever! With absolutely NO fat *or* sugar! *Whatsoever*! (Drip, drip, drip)

(Crap!) That isn't just Hubby, drooling while napping on the sofa! That dripping is coming from the *kitchen!* Right below the upstairs *shower! (Crap!!)* This also happens to be right above our new Chinese-made range! This, of course, has ELECTRICITY in it! *(Crap!!!)*

Because this might possibly involve work, Hubby's of course nowhere to be found. So, I, being fairly handy around the house, decide to take action and immediately run to the neighbor's house, in order to report the problem.

Our neighbor is a typical young and healthy male, with a typical young hard body and typical dark, lush, wavy hair. Not to mention his typical hypnotically Azure eyes!

He's also named, get this, LEVI (oooh, ahhhh!), which I think really fits him perfectly. As does his name.

After mentioning to him how sorry I was, about leaving the dog poo in his front yard, and, yes, *of course,* I'll be sure to pick it up next time! (all the while lost in his Azure eyes), I then invited him to my next book signing and photo shoot, complimented him on his jeans, and went home.

(Drip, drip, drip) *(Crap!)* I'd been so caught up in Mr. Hard-jean's eyes, that I'd completely forgotten to mention the now seemingly *imminent* fire!!! *(Crap!)*

Again thinking quickly, I went upstairs to brush my hair, just in case I'd need to move in with Levi.

I'd just finished packing my suitcase, when I heard Hubby finally come in, from wherever the heck it is, that he's been hiding out for all of these years.

We've lived in the same house for nearly our entire marriage, and after all of that time I *still* have absolutely no idea where it is that he goes! I've often wondered if he's indeed invented the first working cloaking-device, and is actually sitting right in front of me on the sofa. That would certainly explain some of the odors that come from that direction.

Anyway, within fairly short order he was calmly, and competently handling the situation, by spewing forth a very loud string of expletives, that I won't repeat here, (this being a "Favorite Family Book! Great for All Ages!" and all). Suffice it to say, that most of them began with the letter F.

"Well, it looks like the bathroom needs to be gutted" he says, "the tile has separated from the wall, and there's just no other way to fix it".

He's looking a little pastier than usual; I wonder if maybe he's going to throw-up from the possibility of having to do any work. "I'm going to start calling contractors to get bids", he says, "I think this is a job for the pros".

"Nonsense" I say, "Avatar very thoughtfully saved us the last episode of 'This Old House - Bathrooms without Straining'. She must have somehow *known* that we'd need it! What a grand miracle, that she came into our family!"

"Anyway, they'll walk us through it, step by step. Why should we pay someone else to do it?!" (And risk that I may have to get a JOB, in order to pay for it). "God! I'm going to the bar!" he says. "Fine!" I smartly retort.

The next morning I'm awakened by very loud and shrill screaming (which of course I was a having a hard time sleeping through), so I walked out of the bedroom to tell him to "keep it down assh_le! I'm sleeping!" just in time to see Hubby running madly away from the offending leaky bathroom, shrieking much like a schoolgirl, if she were being forced to wear non-designer jeans to school.

He's flailing around wildly, while crazily waving his bathrobe over his head (much like I imagine a matador might do, if he were indeed running *away* from the bull), this, in turn, gave me a less than sexy glimpse of his, ahem, little boys, the image of which still haunts me to this day.

It turns out that, after several beers at the bar (and a good cry), he'd decided to 'buck up, and take on the bathroom job with gusto!' (Translation: I'll need to go the liquor store to stock up on beer).

It also seems that he'd vowed to get an early start on the bathroom demolition. "First thing in the morning!" he'd sworn to the bartender! (Like *he* really gave a crap, one way or another.)

To his credit, I'll admit that he *did* get an early start, since it was 4 friggin o'clock in the morning! This at least explained his lack of daywear, if not his lack of undies.

Now, Hubby knows, as all handy red-blooded American men do, that the first part of *any* good home improvement job is to immediately find your sledgehammer (or better yet, borrow one from LEVI), after all, that had been thoroughly covered, on last week's episode, 'This Old House - Sledgehammers Are Our Friends'.

So, feeling bold, confident, and mostly pretty drunk, his first task was, of course, to 'obliterate those mother-f_ckin tiles!' to make sure they'd *never* hurt us again! What a great idea!

Unfortunately, on his very first swing his "balance was a tad off, and the hammer kind of got away from him", as he says. (Sure. Nice story, beer-boy.)

Not only had he obliterated the mother-f_ckers!, as he'd intended, but he'd also managed to obliterate a large section of the mother-f_ckin exterior wall too (which, I assume, will now never hurt us again).

Regrettably this particular scenario *hadn't* been covered on said TOH episode, so Hubby was now studying the situation (more drinking), while at the same time thinking, "Hmm, what would *Norm* do?" (Yeah, right. As if Norm would dream of working at 4:00a.m., let alone in his bathrobe!) As it happened, he didn't have long to drink, er, I mean think about it.

What happened next was made even more tragic, simply because of the other episodes Hubby hadn't yet had a chance to watch!

'This Old House - Wearing The Proper Undergarments for the Job', not to mention, 'This Old House – How to Safely Remove the Wasps from Your Exterior Walls'.

He's now covered in Donald Duck bandages, and we hired a contractor the next day…

The good news, is, that we'll now have a picture window in the shower. The bad news is for poor LEVI, who lives across from said window.

Springers... You know who you are!

Today's To-Do

- Walgreens (buy bandages) – check
- Pet Store (buy video on home animal grooming techniques) - check
- Make a Batch of Homemade Fudge - check
- Apply Bandages to Burns and Throw out Fudge - check
- Another Dog Walk and Poo Patrol – check
- Write Next Chapter for Best Selling Book - check
- Nap – check

It's 1:30p.m. Time for the Trash!

"If a man sleeps with his mother-in-law, after sleeping with her cousin, who slept with her uncle (in a three-way with his 'hilariously stereotypical neighbor'), does that make him his own son?

These! And other deep questions! Answered today! On SPRINGER!!"

("JERRY, JERRY, JERRY, JERRY, JERRY, JERRY, JERRY, JERRY!")

Now I really don't want to be one of those politically incorrect folks, who'd ignorantly classify good, honest, hardworking people into *any* one particular group, (especially since I'm so much prettier and smarter, than they are), but, again, let's be real about it.

I can't possibly be the only one who's thinking that these people have very likely not only been 'eighty-sixed' from both of the Tulsa Wal-Marts for not keeping to their 'high standards', but are also not considered to be 'Jesse Barnes Seaventh Heven Trailer Park and Bait Emporium' material, mostly because of local health codes.

From what I've seen, shopping at Wal-Mart, (which of course was *only* done as research for this chapter) it would appear that you pretty much just need a name and face, in order to qualify for their 'Elite' customer card (which gets you a free glazed doughnut every time you buy any 2 cans of Sam's Best Quality Ol' Roy dog food)!

Just exactly how low would you have to go, to get banned from there?

As far as Jesse's Trailer Park and Bait Emporium, Jesse's quoted as saying, "I goes out of ma way to help thees peple out, but, durn it, we just *gots* to have standrds!".

It's not that I don't think these are fine, upstanding folks, who go to church on Sundays, while supporting their local library and also fighting against landmines. But, somewhere along the line, between choir practice and the swap meet, they also decided that not only would it be a *great* idea to go on TV for a public flogging (I mean interview), so she can discuss her 14 children with 15 different fathers, but it'd also be an even *greater* idea to be sure to remove most of her clothing before beating the crap out of at least 13 of the fathers during the course of said show. You know, just in case Vogue's watching.

Here's a 46 minute breakdown of the latest programming torture I endured, as part of my research for this book. (Author's Note: I have to confess that I have absolutely no idea what the actual topic was, due to the network censor's incessant beeping, but it doesn't really matter. This pretty well sums it up, every day, I think.)

15 minutes - (JERRY, JERRY, JERRY, JERRY!)

15 minutes - Story line and character (er, I mean guest) introductions. Along with the attending BOO!'s, YOU SUCK!'S, and YO MAMA'S UGLY!'s, and, of course, the network censor's nonstop beeping.

15 minutes - Characters (er, I mean guests) clawing, spitting, and swearing (more beeping) at each other (as well as tearing any remaining clothes off), while the attending Security Guards try *helplessly* to stop the bedlam (after all, someone could get sued after getting hit by a big floppy breast). Sometimes a few pretty good punches do get thrown, though, prompting the audience, who get caught up in the moment, to start punching each other as well.

1 minute – The touching moment, at the end of it all, where Jerry gives us all 'Something Deep to Think About', regarding today's story (Story? Reeaally?), that we can all mull, and *learn* from, until the next 46 minute torture we're forced to endure while getting our oil changed, because we can't reach the friggin' TV!!

Reality Shows (are they really alien messages?)

Today's To-Do

- Bank Withdrawal (pray that the utility check will float for just a few days) - check
- Liquor Store (write check for large bottle of Vodka) - check
- Clean up Mess from Broken Vodka Bottle - check
- Apply Bandages to Cuts and Scrapes - check
- Another Dog Walk and Poo Patrol – check
- Write Next Chapter for Best Selling Book - check
- Nap – check

It's 2:30p.m. Time to get real!

I really have to admit, that I've watched what's probably way more than my share of reality TV. I should also admit, that I'm currently attending a 12-step program, as a part of my recovery (mentioning it in this book is step 1).

While it's definitely been an ongoing monkey on my back, at least I can say, if nothing else, that, with my great knowledge and experience on this subject, this chapter really shouldn't take more than about 1 minute, 30 seconds to write (or so), so I probably don't have to worry about missing anything important on Springer.. (I mean C-Span Congress Coverage. Yeah, that's it.)

Over the years I've watched all of them, from 'Trapped Celebrities on Bikini Island' to 'Real World Boston – When Will They Puke?', and there's just something sadistically compelling about them, that I find hard to resist. One of my all-time favorites is, 'Survivor – Mostly Naked in Paradise'.

Maybe it's how they manage to even find these otherwise good, normal (and I'm sure God-fearing), church-going folks, that become *so* caught up in getting their 15 minutes of mediocre fame, that they'll not *only* risk getting MALARIA and EBOLA, (certainly bad enough), but, that they're *also* willing to sleep underneath the sweaty fat guy in the flea-ridden dirt, and to eat large tropical beetles (mmm..tastes like chicken). All while also fighting off poisonous snakes, and Jeff Probst.

Just to win that week's immunity idol, (also known as another opportunity to go yet *another* week without a bath) and a very remote possibility of winning the $1million bucks, which of course comes along with a federal prison term for tax evasion.

Yes, I'm quite impressed with their spirit, and the many hardships they must face!

Such as whether or not the Nordstrom's string bikini actually *is* just a BIT too small, after all?

And, whether or not it will actually keep her boobs covered (while still looking young and perky), during the next immunity challenge (which, coincidentally, requires them to hang upside down).

They can have it. I like my comfort, my showers, and my boobs will never be young and perky again anyway.

Another favorite is 'Catfish Noodling!', where some guy named Bubba goes after 'Today's Catch', for his 'Bubba's BBQ and Bait Emporium', by sticking his entire fist into the first open mouth he finds underwater, at the nearby gravel pit.

If he's indeed *lucky* enough that it clenches back on, much like I imagine a mechanical vice might do, then "Him and the Kin'll be Eatin Good Tonight!"

One show I haven't seen, though, and one I believe would not only be a SUPER MEGA-HIT ($$$$$$), but would undeniably be the biggest challenge of them all! 'Survivor Housewife! – Can she really do it all, and still look like Barbie?'

This hit program would include such challenges as: 'Creative cooking for 6 – With nothing but a bag of rice, chocolate pudding, and 3 cans of Spam', 'Laundry for 6 - after a week of eating nothing but rice, chocolate pudding, and canned Spam', and finally, my personal favorite, 'Staying Fashionably Shaved, with a Colicky Baby'.

Any woman that can actually *meet* these challenges (no time limit required, as they really don't expect anyone to actually complete them), will go on to become the network's 'Queen for a Day!'

This exciting package includes such prizes, as: 'A Clean Shirt (Vomit-Free)!' valued at over $200! 'A Good Night's Sleep (Baby AND Hubby Free)!', valued at over $1000!. Not to mention, 'A Long (and solo) Vacation in Las Vegas) 'Invaluable!'

THEN I'll be impressed!

Game Shows. I'll take the 'NEW CAR', Bob!!

Today's To-Do

- Back to Liquor Store (write another check) - check
- Walgreens (more bandages) - check
- Have a Cocktail – check
- Clean and Sanitize Good China – check
- Apply Bandages to Cuts and Scrapes - check
- Another Dog Walk and Poo Patrol – check
- Write Next Chapter for Best Selling Book - check
- Nap – check

It's 3:30p.m. Time to play!

LET'S! PLAY! JEOPARDY!!!!

WITH YOUR HOST!! ALEXXX TREBEECCC!!!

ALEX "Welcome, everyone, to the show! Let's get right to it! Contestant 1, please choose the first category!"

CONTESTANT 1 "I'll take 'Constantly-Renamed Geography', Alex, for $200"

ALEX "I'm known as the *Largest Japanese Island"*

(LORI "What is Chinatown?".. BUZZ!)

CONTESTANT 1 "What is Honshu?"

ALEX "Correct! Next category!"

CONTESTANT 1 "'Immaterial Science', Alex, for $200"

ALEX "I'm known as the number of feet, in a *fathom*"

(LORI "What is five?".. BUZZ!)

CONTESTANT 2 "What is Five, Alex?"

ALEX "Sorry, incorrect", "it's six." "*Six.*" (What a *moron*!) "Next category please!"

CONTESTANT 1 "I'll take Immaterial Science, again, ALEX, for $400"

ALEX "I'm *also* known as '*room temperature*'"…"room temp-er-a-ture!"

(LORI "With or without hot flashes?"..BUZZ!)

CONTESTANT 3 "What is 68 degrees, Alex?"

ALEX "Correct! On to the final category!"

CONTESTANT 3 "Okay, Music, for $200, Alex"

ALEX "*I'm* known as '*Bobtail*' in the classic holiday song, '*Jingle Bells*'"

(LORI "Who is Santa's (ahem!) '*favorite*' elf?"…BUZZ!)

CONTESTANT 3 "What is a horse, Alex?"

ALEX "Correct CONTESTANT 3! You're today's champion!

ALEX "CONTESTANT 3 you've *soundly* crushed CONTESTANT 1's and CONTESTANT 2's asses" (*not to mention Lori's*), "and will return again tomorrow, for your chance" (*very* remote chance) "at winning the $1 million dollar top Jeopardy prize!!"

Okay, I suck at this game, let's try another.

ARE YOU SMARTER THAN A 5TH GRADER!?

WITH YOUR HOST! JEFFFF FOXWORTHYYYY!!

Read the sentence. Look for the phrase that completes the sentence correctly.

The team _____ play baseball.

Answers:

a. did not want
b. refusing to

c. would really rather 'party hearty', than
d. loved to

LORI "That answer would be 'C', Jeff, they'd rather party hearty."

JEFF FOXWORTHY "Oh! I'm so sorry, Lori!!! It's actually 'D', 'loved to!'" "Let's try again!"

Read the question. Find the phrase with correct punctuation.

Which is the correct way to close a letter?

Answers:

a. Up Yours
b. Yours truly,
c. Yours Truly:
d. Yours truly

LORI "I believe that'd be 'A', Jeff."

JEFF FOXWORTHY "Oh, I'm SO sorry LORI! There went your chance at the $1Million Dollars! But you still have a chance for our second place prize! A new World Globe, with the very latest of the constantly renamed countries.

Select the best answer.

The Second Continental Congress chose _____ to lead the Continental Army.

Answers:

a. John Adams
b. Barack Obama
c. Benedict Arnold
d. George Washington

LORI "I just know that must be 'B' Jeff"

JEFF "So sorry, again! That is incorrect! The answer is 'Benedict Arnold'. That's BEEN-IID-ICCT ARRRR-NOLLD!!!" (*Moron!*).

"Thanks so much, though, for being on the show! We'll see you again next week, on the newest of our challenging programs, 'See Dick Read, See Jane Run. *Can* They Catch Up?'"

Sigh. Okay, one more.

WHEEL! OF! FORTUNE!!

WITH YOUR HOST! PATTT SAJAKKK!! AND YOUR *FAVORITE* LETTER TURNER! VANNNNA WHIIITE!!

PAT "Lori, if you can solve this puzzle, you'll be our $1million dollars, TOP WHEEL PRIZE winner!!!!!!"

'FL_CK   _F   GEESE'

LORI "FLECK IF GEESE!!! "FLECK IF GEESE!!"

PAT "Oh, I'm so sorry!!!" "I'm afraid the answer was FLOCK OF GEESE, *FLOCK OF* GEESE!" (*Moron!*)

"Let's all give her a big hand anyway, folks! Thanks so very much for playing!"

VANNA WHITE (Smiling) (Clap, clap, clap!!)

Fine. I've got better things to watch anyway.

Nature shows. See Thumper. See Tigger. See Tigger eat.

Today's To-Do

- Water Flowers and Shrubs - check
- Fertilize Lawn - check
- Spray Bee-hive next to Garage - check
- Apply Bandages to Bee Stings – check
- Another Dog Walk and Poo Patrol – check
- Write Next Chapter for Best Selling Book - check
- Nap – check

It's 4:00p.m. Time for Nature!

Let me say, first off, that I am a *huge* fan of mother-nature and her many, many splendors!

For instance, I spend hours and hours, snacking on the sofa in my feety pajamas, enjoying God's many varied, and wondrous creatures on such fine programs, as, 'Wildebeests, How Far Can They Really Fly?' and 'Baby Seals, They're Mmmm..Good!' Or, one of my very favorites, 'Gorillas and Man – A Very Hairy Relationship'.

From my very (very) comfortable sofa (with built in drink holders and wine fridge), I've been able to travel the world!

I've been from London's Rift Continent, to Japan's Chinatown, and everywhere in between! All done with virtually NO possibility of the threats normally linked with world travel; such as nasty scrapes, blisters, or killer bees! Not to mention the Rattlesnakes, Hanta-virus, and, perhaps the worst of all, smeared mascara!

Nope I'll stay on the sofa to see the world, thanks very much. I'm a city girl, and we have electricity, showers and cable, here in the city.

My love for nature began at a young age. I remember how, on Sunday evenings at 6:00, the entire family would gather around our 'SEVEN AND A HALF INCH QUAZAR TELEVISION - NOW IN *COLOR!!!*' (yes, we w*ere* billionaires, in case you were wondering), to watch this week's episode of 'Mutual Of Omaha's Wild Kingdom!', with our expert guides Marlin Perkins and Jim Fowler, who take us into the 'deep and dangerous wilderness', with nothing but their courage, their gumption, and, most importantly, their camera-man.

 MARLIN "Today, we're going to extract semen from an endangered River Constrictor, known to be one of the *most aggressive* predators in the world, to take back to our zoo for analysis."

DAD "What the hell happened to the piece of foil?!! That I had attached to the rabbit-ears?!! GOD-D_MN IT!!", "MARTHA!! BRING ME THE ALUMINUM FOIL!!"

LITTLE BROTHER "I needed it to make a space helmet for my gerbil" (suddenly breaking out in tears)

MARLIN "This fella's over 100 feet long, so we expect him to be a *pretty* tough customer!" (sharing a laugh with Jim)

DAD "MARTHA!!!" (Turning beet red, with one eye twitching wildly)

LITTLE SISTER "Daddy, would you like to hear the song that I wrote for you?" "I call it 'Let's kill a six-pack'"

JIM "Marlin, this is *by far* one of the most dangerous jobs we've attempted", "One wrong move could mean serious injury or worse!"

DAD "SH_T! MARTHA!!!

LITTLE BROTHER "Now little Gerby won't wake *up*!" (Crying harder)

LITTLE SISTER (singing) "Daddy's home, I love to see, but why does he smell so *funny*?"

MARLIN "Yes, you're right Jim, let's get this over with!" (They head into the water)

LITTLE SISTER (singing) "You pick him off the floor"

LITTLE BROTHER "I HATE ALL OF YOU!" (Runs, screaming, from the room)

MARLIN "Uh oh, Jim, he's got a hold of my leg!"

LITTLE SISTER (singing) "Then bails him out on Sunday"

JIM "He's got me too Marlin!" "He's trying to pull me under!!"

LITTLE SISTER (singing) "Until next weekend comes!"

MARLIN "This isn't looking good!!!" "Jim!!!"

DAD "What is that, they're fighting with? Everything's a blur!!" "Is that a Duckbilled Platypus?", "Oh no! There goes the horizontal hold!!"

JIM "MARLIN!" (Struggling, splashing, and grunting)

MARLIN "Glug, glug"

CAMERAMAN "Oh My God!!!" "Get the producer on the phone!!"

DAD "D_MN it! What's going on!! I can't see *anything*!!"

MOM (swallowing a Valium, while staggering into the room) "Quit your f_cking hollering! I TOLD YOU! We're out of f_cking foil!!"

DAD (*both* eyes now twitching wildly) "F_CK IT THEN! I'M GOING TO THE BAR!"

MOM "GOOD!! DON'T WORRY ABOUT COMING BACK EITHER!"

DAD (storming out the front door) "B_TCH!"

MOM (giving Dad the 2-finger salute) "ASSH_LE!"

LITTLE SISTER (singing) "And that's why his nose is red!"

Yup, I love nature shows!

Real Housewives (and other snotty bitches)

Today's To-Do

- Plan Dinner - check
- Pound Meat and put in Marinade Sauce - check
- Clean up Dropped Meat on Floor (what dog missed) - check
- Microwave Swanson's Hungry Man Dinners – check
- Cleanup Dog Puke – check
- Cleanup Hubby Puke - check
- Another Dog Walk and Poo Patrol – check
- Write Next Chapter for Best Selling Book - check
- Nap – check

It's 5:30p.m. Time for the Housewives!

A Day in the Life, of a Hollywood Housewife

- Wake up to the aroma of fresh lavender, with a somewhat *musky* undertone, and the gentle touch of Sven, your gorgeous personal Swedish masseuse.
- Breakfast and morning paper, on the palatial veranda overlooking the Caribbean Sea, while Sven rubs, um,

various pressure points, through all five wonderful courses.
- Hot bubble bath, while on the phone with Housewife 2, during which a *terrible* fight erupts, over who'll get the 'just now opened up' appointment with celebrity facialist, Dr. Bernstein, at 10:00.
- Appointment with Dr. Bernstein at 10:00.
- Another massage. Mmmmm! Yummy!
- Makeup and hair (a grueling process which requires several cocktails, along with an inordinate amount of censor beeping).
- Nap (after all, it's been a *busy* day!).
- Touch up makeup and hair (another cocktail).
- Lunch, and the Daily Vogue, again on the veranda. Another phone conversation, this time with Housewife 3, during which a *terrible* fight erupts, over who'll get the 'just now opened up' appointment for a foot scraping, with celebrity podiatrist Dr. Goldberg, at 3:00.
- Dr. Goldberg, at 3:00.
- Bikini Wax (Brazilian please!).
- Another Massage (who wouldn't?!).
- Dress For Dinner (With your personal assistant, Amanda, who dresses you and brushes your teeth).
- Dinner on the veranda, with the Daily Enquirer. No phone conversation this time, all words are, by now, slurred and incomprehensible.
- Nap (for obvious reasons).
- Makeup and hair (again for obvious reasons).

- Party with other D-list celebrity's, who are *also* looking to get a featured episode on the latest 'Celebrity Rehab with Dr. Drew'.
- Another Bikini wax (we like to keep her tidy!).
- Dessert on the veranda, with the Daily People, and one final rub from Sven, before climbing into your luxurious bed, and a beautifying night's sleep, wearing the $5000 night cream made from baby seal fat.

A Day in the Life, of a Working Housewife

- Wake up to the aroma of last night's boiled cabbage, with an almost *fishy* undertone, along with the gentle touch of Hubby's Chubby, which is placed firmly between your butt cheeks.
- Breakfast at the bus stop, (because your car came down with case of shingles, or something mechanical like that), with the morning paper that you found on the ground, next to the used condom.
- After being splashed by a car that looked suspiciously like a Hollywood Housewife's private limo, you follow up with a string of 'F' words, and have a good cry.
- You receive a complimentary massage, from a homeless groper on the bus.
- Retouch makeup and hair (for obvious reasons).
- Pop 2 No-Doze and drink 3 diet sodas.

- Suddenly remember, during the morning meeting with the top brass, that you forgot to bring tampons to work today. Big mistake!!
- Eat lunch on the bus, on the way to Wal-Mart to get tampons, while reading the comically altered billboards, placed above the comically altered windows.
- More No-Doze, more sodas.
- Suddenly remember, during the afternoon meeting with the top brass, that, even, $81.63 later, you *still* forgot to buy the freakin tampons! GOD!!!
- Eat a stale, 'bottom of the purse' Milky Way bar, on the bus, on the way back to Wal-Mart.
- Receive another relaxing massage, this time from Casper, the friendly rat, that's unfortunately taken up residence in the seat next to you.
- Return home and dress for dinner (i.e., wait for your ratty sweats to warm up in the dryer, while rinsing out the nasty 2 year old pair of panty-hose that you keep forgetting to replace, no matter *how* many times you go to Wal-Mart.)
- More No-Doze and soda.
- Clean the disgusting green gick, from the bathroom sink. Vow to *never* ask what it is.
- Vow to get a bikini wax, REAL SOON!
- 8-9 hours of quality TV time.
- Screw the brushing and flossing.

- Exhaustedly clean up the saltine crackers and dog hair from the bed, then on to some *much* needed sleep! Preferably before Hubby's Chubby wakes up again.

A Day in the Life, of a Recently Retired Housewife

- Wake up around 10:00 or so, the aroma of Hubby's recycled cabbage, from last night, still lingering in the air (even though he's been gone for at least 3 hours).
- Breakfast on the sofa, while circling want ads in the paper to show good intentions of finding a new job.
- A good cry. Those adorable puppy for-sale ads *really* get to me!
- Receive relaxing massage from our small leg humping dog.
- After an hour give up on makeup and hair, have another good cry.
- Pop a Vicodin, and drink 3 sodas.
- Go to Wal-Mart, to buy tampons and Hubby's hemorrhoid cream.
- Lunch on sofa, while reading paper insert from hemorrhoid cream.
- Nap (who wouldn't?).
- Realize that you forgot tampons. Back to Wal-Mart
- Dress for dinner, by covering huge nose zit with a Donald Duck bandage.

- Dinner on sofa, reading paper insert from band aid.
- More Vicodin and soda.
- 14-16 hours of TV.
- F_ck the green gick in the bathroom sink.
- F_ck the Bikini wax.
- F_ck the saltines and dog hair. Maybe tomorrow.

The Doctors. Curing *Your* Disease! R*iiiiigh*t after the Break!

Today's To-Do

- Cleanup Dinner Mess – check
- Prepare and Put Brownies in the Oven for Dessert - check
- Have a Cocktail - check
- Have another Cocktail - check
- Throw away Burnt Brownies – check
- Another Dog Walk and Poo Patrol – check
- Write Next Chapter for Best Selling Book - check
- Nap – check

6:30p.m. Time to Heal!

An intensely sore mouth (Jell-O shots are way more painful than usual), with high fever (do hot flashes count?), soon to be followed by a fire-like sore throat, and swollen lymph nodes, roughly the size of a tennis ball. Excessive drooling is usually present, (especially after 10 Jell-O shots).

*(R'uh R'oh! I've got **all** of those!)*

Narrowed and constricted airways, with symptoms such as barking cough, a raspy hoarse voice, and a harsh, 'grating' noise when breathing. The cough is very distinctive (and annoying to most spouses), often compared with the sound of a barking seal.

(Oh crap! Those too!)

Patches of chronically itchy, dry, lizard like skin, usually on the hands, neck, face, arms, torso or legs (really, where else *is* there?). Soon to be followed by, yellowish to light brown crusty, or pus-filled blisters, which will then, in turn, break and ruin your brand new blouse.

(Check!!)

Chronic widespread pain (may even spread to spouse) that affects the right and left side of the body (exactly what other sides *are* there?), above and below the waist (okay, someone's just trying to increase their word count here). Feels pain in at least 17 of 18 possible tender points, nine on one side of the body, nine on the other, when light pressure is applied. (I've got it, in 47 out of 18).

(Oh, Good Lord!!! I'm not well!!)

(Quick! I'd better turn on the TV!!!)

"Today, on Doctor Oz! We're going to tell the *heart-wrenching* story of a Korean Orphan, and her long pilgrimage to find her adoptive parents!" (Oh, no! Not this freakin' kid again!)

"This *very* brave young girl survived an ocean journey of over 2000 miles! *And*, get this! With *only* her Donald Duck inflatable water wings keeping her afloat!" [Cut to girl] "It was scary!"

"Then we'll tell you the nutritional tips, that allowed this amazing little girl to make that *incredible journey!*" (Well, that's some new and useful information, at least)

"Then, we're going to show you the *best* brownie recipe ever! With absolutely NO fat *or* sugar! *Whatsoever!*" (Oh, for Pete's Sake! Can't they come up with *anything* original to say?)

Well this doesn't seem like much of a medical show to me!! Every person there seems to be fit, trim and healthy, with continued access to a good self-tanning cream.

Not a thing like the disgusting, coughing, germ-infested folks that I see at *my* doctor's office! And the patients are even worse!

And, why the heck does this guy need to wear scrubs on the show, anyway? Is he planning on doing some kind of open-heart surgery, right after the break?

Why he doesn't even have a stethoscope! Which, as all of us who grew up with 'Marcus Welby, M.D.', know, is the one thing that any good Dr. needs!

I don't trust this guy; I'm getting a second opinion!

"Today, on the Doctors! We're going to tell the *heart-wrenching* story of an overweight man, and his long, arduous journey, to get to his current 'fighting weight' of 680lbs!"

"This *very* brave man survived an emotional and physical journey of over 20 pounds! *And*, get this! With *only* 8 meals a day, to keep his energy going!" [Cut to man] "It was scary!" (Why this sounds suspiciously like the story of the Korean girl, only with a few key words replaced!)

"Then, we're going to show you the *best* brownie recipe ever! With absolutely NO fat *or* sugar! *Whatsoever!*" (Good Lord, some writers just have *no* shame!)

Oh Brother. I'll just pay the bill, and see a real doctor! At least *he* can prescribe pills!

Infomercials and you. Yes, you really *can* change the channel!

Today's To-Do

- Dig out 2 year old Girl Scout Cookies for Dessert – check
- Cleanup Dropped Cookies (missed by dog) - check
- Cleanup Dog Puke – check
- Watch Cat Eat what I'd Missed - check
- Watch Cat Eat His Own Puke - check
- Another Cocktail - check
- Forget about Dog Walk and Poo Patrol – check
- Cleanup Dog Poo in Living-room - check
- Write Next Chapter for Best Selling Book - check
- Nap – check

7:30p.m. Time to Shop!

"Thanks for tuning in to today's program, where we're going to introduce you to the *amazing* health and beauty benefits, of the *Total Home Gym!*"

Christie Brinkley
Model, actress, and mother of three

Christie Brinkley, one of America's most successful and blondest models, has been committed to health and beauty her entire life.

For over 10 years she has relied on Total Gym for a youthful figure, as well as a steady retirement income.

The total body workout she gets from the Total Gym helps to shape a leaner, slimmer, look while building strength, increasing her energy level and doubling her investment return.

Christie has even developed some Pilates moves on the Total Gym that are *just* as effective as the Pilates Torture Stretch, but with 'up to one third less' torture!

"Unlike any other piece of equipment in the world, the Total Gym is effective, fast, fun and easy. I have never used any other piece of equipment in the world that has been so effective, so fast, so fun, and so easy!"

"The Total Gym will get you into shape, and bump up my bank account, faster than you would ever think possible!"

"Once you try it, you'll be hooked for life! Try it today!"

Chuck Norris
Author, actor, action star, and martial artist

Chuck's past low paying jobs demanded that he stay in *top*

financial shape, that's why Total Gym was the only piece of home fitness equipment Chuck Norris ever sold!

For 30 years he's endorsed Total Gym because he has seen, first-hand, what a tremendous difference this machine makes to anyone who wants to build muscle, lose weight, and increase Chuck's bank account.

"What attracted me to the Total Gym 30 years ago is the same reason I still sell it today. It delivers *some* results. But, more importantly, a pretty nice paycheck too! I have more money now, than I ever did when I was starring in those terrible B-movies!"

"But, let's be honest. No one, *especially* me, actually likes (or actually does), exercise! So, for the next 25 minutes we'll be watching Christy's body double demonstrate this *amazing* machine!

"As for me, I'm going shopping for an 'assist chair' that'll pull me up whenever I need to get a beer. Then I'm heading over to the Krispy-Kreme."

Why they LOVE their Total Gym!

Quick & saves time - I can get a Total Gym royalty check in as little as 5 days! That's all it takes!

Savings - I've been using my Total Gym for over 3 years! I would have spent so much *more* with a monthly gym membership, especially since I got mine for free!

Results - I'm in the best financial shape of my life, thanks to Total Gym!

Versatility - With over 80 exercises, there's always something new to try on the Total Gym! And we get a royalty for all of them!

Usability - Everyone in my family can use the money that I make!

Easy on my joints - Saves my body from unwanted and unnecessary stress to the joints, by paying for my liposuction!

Portability – Easy to hide out of sight. Just like the royalty checks!

Convenience - It's right in my home so I don't have to drive anywhere, or wait for any machines. Plus, I have direct deposit!

Achievement - The Total Gym makes me feel like I've accomplished something that makes me feel great! I really love my new Jaguar!

Unique - I can mimic any exercise from the gym on the Total Gym, and I also get a generous annual bonus!

Wow, They both look great!! WE MUST HAVE IT!!!

"God, I've seen complete custom car kits come packed in smaller boxes than this!" Hubby says, looking helplessly at the shipment, lying at the end of the driveway.

"I thought you said this was a *home gym*! This looks more like something you'd use to load elephants into the circus trucks!", he bellows, "God, what were you thinking?!"

"I was thinking that maybe if I looked like Christy Brinkley that I'd finally be able to find someone with finances like Chuck Norris!" I reply smartly, while inside I'm wondering too, what *was* I thinking?!

We can't even lift the box to get it into the garage, let alone all the way to the basement (where it will have to live, so we won't feel guilty about it sitting unused every day)!

How many drinks had I had, anyway, when I'd ordered the stupid thing?

"Maybe we can carry it down in several pieces, since it looks like it might need a bit of assembly" I offer helpfully, a bit alarmed by the hateful look in his eyes. "I've seen complete custom car kits that require less f_ckin assembly!" he says, more than a tad spitefully.

"This is the f_ckin most ridiculous thing you've ever bought!" he adds, just to make sure I get his less than enthusiastic response to the whole idea.

"You won't feel that way at all, once I look like Christy! After all, Billy Joel wrote a number one hit song about her" I say, while thinking that he'd probably write one about me too.

"Christy is a MODDDDEL, she's PRETTTYYY!" he snipes, like I really need him to sound out the words. "When are you going to start living in the real world?!" he adds, somewhat pleadingly.

"That's only because she has more money!" I snap, absolutely sure that it's the truth. "She gets to buy all the designer clothes, get the best spa treatments, and the top personal celebrity stylists!" I cry, "All that *I'm* asking is to be able to at least use her celebrity gym!"

I give Hubby my very best pout, which, based on Hubby's reaction, must have resembled the 'Billy Bass singing fish' just around mid-song. He gives in anyway, because, well, he knows it's just a whole lot easier to put the thing together, than it would be to argue about it.

Two hours of beer, cursing, and general misery later, he now sat in front of a large pile of hardware that probably resembled the Space Shuttle, as it was *before* they actually built it.

"Can I help at all?" I ask, genuinely concerned that he might divorce me over this, and I'll have to get a JOB. "How about a good shot of something stiff, to get you motivated?"

Looking more than a bit evil, he says, "get me a stiff crow bar, and I'll give *something* a good shot alright!"

I decide it's time to get out of his way, and cook him a delicious dinner.

"You've got to bend it around the corner!" I say the next morning, after our Total Gym is finally now in one piece.

"Exactly how do you propose that we *bend* a f_ckin eleven foot piece of steel around a corner?" he hollers, "just lift up on your end!"

"I can't move it", I say breathlessly, already 'Totally' fed up with working out on our 'Total' Gym, "it just won't budge!"

"Well it's certainly not going to be very useful sitting here under the pool table, now is it?" he says, scornfully. "You knew that it had to fit into the other room, didn't you think to check the measurements?!" he adds loudly, again to make sure that I'm totally aware of his displeasure over the whole thing.

"Well, didn't *you* think to either? You know, BEFORE you put the whole f_ckin thing together??!!" I say, politely, ready to make a run for it if he decides to pull out a crow bar.

After a few days of blissful silence from Hubby, and his sleeping on the couch, I was ready to admit that, perhaps, I *had* showed a bit of poor judgment in thinking that I'll ever look like Christy, and that maybe my measuring skills weren't quite up to snuff, after all.

After a night at the bar Hubby agreed, and is now under the

pool table, disassembling the colossal and vile beast.

I'm on hold with FedEx, waiting to schedule a pickup.

Auctions and you. Do you REALLY have a big enough garage?

Today's To-Do

- Catch up on Chin Hairs - check
- Catch up on, ahem, Personal Shaving – check
- Apply Bandages to Cuts and Scratches - check
- Another Cocktail - check
- Hubby to do Dog Walk and Poo Patrol – check
- Write Next Chapter for Best Selling Book (likely the worst, yet) - check
- Nap – check

8:00p.m. Time to Bid!

As part of our time, energy, and money saving strategy, one thing Hubby and I especially enjoy together is the weekly Saturday night auto auction on TV, "Proudly Sponsored" by our *good* friends at Budweiser!

Hubby loves them for the cool cars and hot action, but, mostly, he loves them for the bodacious beer babes, which, coincidentally, are *also* provided by our good friends over there at Budweiser.

I love the auction, too, mainly because I get a chance to drink wine and read uninterrupted. But, even more importantly, because Hubby *doesn't* know the phone number to call in and bid. (I'd actually paid a technician to specially calibrate the TV screen size, to guarantee that it would never be seen by Hubby, due to the great financial harm that would obviously come from it.) I *really* thought that we were safe.

"The BIG one's coming to town!" Hubby says, squealing like a schoolgirl, if she were just asked to the prom, by the school's star quarterback, "I got LUCKY and found tickets in the SECOND row!"

He looks ecstatic, but also a bit pasty, like he may throw-up from the anticipation of it all.

"You mean that Cirque De Soleil is *finally* coming to town! Oh, honey! That's Wonderful!" I cry. "You're going to be getting some extra special treatment, tonight, *if* you know what I mean!" attempting my best 'come hither' look, that, from what I gather from Hubby's reaction, must look a bit like an overly lusty Rhinoceros.

"No, no, no, it's the CAR AUCTION!" he gushes, "It's coming NEXT WEEK!", again with the squeal.

"What f_ckin car auction?!!!" I sweetly ask, "I don't want to go to a f_ckin car auction!! We don't have enough f_ckin room for any more cars or motorcycles, not to mention the f_ckin money!!" "Moron!" I add, with a loving smile.

"Well, maybe if you'd think about getting a f_ckin JOB, we wouldn't have to worry so much about money!" he says, a bit less affectionately.

"In the meantime, remember that *I* went with *you*, to the 'Great Quilts of America' exhibition! My stomach was queasy the entire time, wondering if we'd run into someone I know!" he whines, looking decidedly queasy right now, as he relives the terrible memory, "I'd *think* that you can do this *one* thing for me!"

Good Lord, he looked as if he were about to cry! (Sigh) I guess, if it's THAT important to him, okay. (Sigh) (And also if it'll help him to temporarily forget, about my lack of a JOB!)

Unfortunately, by the next week he'd remembered.

"I don't want to park in this lot; they're charging *double* what we can pay, *right* down the street!", he moans, "You know that we don't have the money, since you absolutely refuse to work!" he just had to add.

"Why, it's HIGHWAY ROBBERY!" he shouts suddenly, pounding on the steering wheel as if it were charging him a parking fee, as well.

"I know a much better lot right behind the Bargain Liquor and Check Cashing Palace, and they're a *much* better deal" still screaming.

"But that's like a half mile away, and you insisted that I wear these six inch spike heels here!" I scream back "Do you *really* think that we'll manage to have sex in Bill Clinton's town-car, when no one's looking?" "Moron!" I add, caringly.

"No, what I'm really hoping for is to have sex in the car with one of those bodacious beer-babes, that'll be brought to me by my good friends at Budweiser!" he snaps, spitefully. "I just figured that, with those giant shoes, you won't be able to totter over and bother us!" he says, looking wistful.

By the time I thought of a good comeback (which I never did, by the way), we were already 'decidedly blocked' into Bubba's Bargain Parking Emporium, and I was too exhausted to argue about it.

"You didn't mention that we'd have to climb through f_ckin rose bushes to get here from Bubba's! I think I saw a rattle-snake in there, and I'm pretty sure I there's a hive of some sort too!" "God, you're so f_ckin cheap!" I say, lovingly.

"That's why I'm with *you*, babe", he replies, unpleasantly.

"Okay, fine, we're here. Get me a beer to drink, and one to soak my feet, and I'll be fine. But for God's sake, though, don't do ANYTHING that might be mistaken for a bid!" I say, pleadingly, "I've heard the stories!"

"Of course not, honey. You know that I'd never spend that kind of money, at least when you're sober." he states, sincerely.

(BZZZZ) "Here's your beer, now try to quit griping and just enjoy yourself!!", he says, handing me two Bud Lights. (BZZZZ)

"First up is a *Classic* '69 Hemi! With an Overbearing Engine (BZZZZ) and an Overbearing Price-tag to match!" says the announcer, who looks just like Bob Barker did, in 1973. (BZZZZ)

"We expect this to bring one of the *top prices,* for this event!" Bob says. (BZZZZ)

"Wow, what kind of idiot would pay that much?!" I say, wonderingly. I look at Hubby, who's (BZZZZ) obviously trying to do the math in his head, to decide if we can swing the payments (he looks like he's in pain from all that thinking).

"That's (BZZZZ) just (BZZZZ) crazy!" I say. (BZZZZ)

Bob, "Humin-an-na-an-we-better-buy-buy,-humin-an-na-we-better-buy-buy!" (BZZZZ!)

(BZZZZ!!) What IS that??

OHH, MYY, GODDD!!! There is a HUGE FREAKIN WASP! And it's (BZZZZ!) nestled (tangled) right in my

HAIR! Right next to my EAR! (BZZZZ!) This leads directly into my brain!!!

OHH! MYY! GODDD!!!

Flailing around wildly, I try to remove the creature by creatively using Hubby's hand as a weapon. He promptly jumps away and swats at me, as if *I* were indeed a wasp, and tangled up in *his* hair!

Bob, "Humin-an-na-an-we-better-buy-(BZZZZ) -buy-humin-an-na-we-better-buy-buy!" (BZZZZ!) "We have $65,000 dollars!"

"Sh_t! Get it!" I scream.

Bob, "Humin-an-na-an-we-better-buy-buy-humin-an-na-we-better-buy-buy" (BZZZZ!) "We now have $75,000 dollars!"

"G_d-D_mn It!" Hubby yells, raising his fist. "I don't want to get stung!"

Bob, "Humin-an-na-an-we-better-buy-buy-humin-an-na-we-better-buy-buy" (BZZZZ!!!!) "Folks, we have $80,000 dollars!!" "Can you *believe* (BZZZZ!!!!) this?"

"Aaarrrrgghhh!" I stop, drop and roll, like they taught us in school, (BZZZZ) "It's going to kill me, if I can't get it!"

Bob, "Humin-an-na-an-we-better-buy-buy-humin-an-na-we-better-buy-buy!" He's clearly more excited, now.

"Sold!! For $90,000 dollars!! To the screaming woman on the ground with the massively swollen earlobe!"

"Congratulations!!"

Anyone that's interested in buying a Classic '69 Hemi, please call Hubby at 303-611-1750 (mornings are best). If you want to see it in person, it's parked in the next door neighbor's driveway.

Antique Roadshows. No, Billy Bob, that black velvet matador is *not* an early Van Gough

Today's To-Do

- Catch up on Spam mails - check
- Catch up on Sewing and Mending – check
- Apply Bandages to Cuts and Pokes - check
- Another Cocktail - check
- Last Dog Walk and Poo Patrol – check
- Write Next Chapter for Best Selling Book (heck, let's make it two) - check
- Nap – skipped, too close to bedtime.

9:00p.m. Time for Antiques!

GUEST: (Smiling Brightly, Expectantly) What I *mainly* know is that I *love* them! Because I've collected all of the magazines, that talked about the books!

And then my husband gave me my first London one about 20 years ago, as a Christmas gift, and about ten years ago the Noodle!

APPRAISER: (Smiling Skeptically, Dubiously) Okay then, so *enlighten* us please, with your expertise. Who's the artist here?

GUEST: (Smugly, Assuredly) His name is Ludwig Bemelmans!

APPRAISER: (Condescendingly, Mockingly) Annnd? He is famous forrrr?????

GUEST: (Cocky, Confident) Madeline books!

APPRAISER: (Disappointed, Vile) Right!

GUEST: (Authoritatively, Firmly) Which I would say is the most...

APPRAISER: (Abruptly, Sternly, Threateningly) *The* most recognizable name!

He's a semi-famous illustrator, and a German immigrant, who came to the United States after Ireland's Great Potato Famine in 1898. He's also painted some murals at a bistro that he owned in Paris, some time ago.

So he was into murals, and obviously he was into doing children's illustrations. This is an illustration from one of the books, called Madeline in London. Now, *everybody* knows of Madeline in Paris!

Do *you* know the line in Madeline when it says, "In the middle of the night, "Miss Clavel turned on the light and said, 'Something is not right'"?

GUEST: (Timidly, Quieter) Something is not right?

APPRAISER: (Disdainfully, Jeeringly) Yeah. Well, when I first looked at this, you could *quite* obviously see the *sloppily* hand-applied color, and that the colors start way up here at the British flag!

And, while the white of this here is *obviously* the famous double-decker bus down here, it's *completely* wrong, and certainly done in a *gouache* over-color!

And when we turn to the black lines is when we begin to think that there might be even *more* of an issue here!

I thought to myself, "I think these lines are printed." But it turns out that they're *not*, because once you get them into the right light, you see that there is a graduation in the black. That is... a printed line stays black from end to end and it's the same shade of black.

So that's what putting this in the right light allows us to tell.

GUEST: (Whispering, Apprehensive) Oh?

APPRAISER: (Arrogantly, Self-Importantly) He died in 1962. And in 1961 he finished Madeline in London. So these were probably sold as part of his estate.

He probably never really intended these to go anywhere, which is why he was so careless with what he did, including signing over the white mark down at the bottom. This *could* make it *completely worthless!*

Let's look at this one here. Tell me what you think you know about this one!

GUEST: (Fearful, Nervous) Well, uh, I *think*, this was *maybe* done as an illustration for somebody else's book?

APPRAISER: (Non-committal, Evasive) Okay.

GUEST: (Tentative, Tense) And... But I, I *do* know that he loved dachshunds himself..

APPRAISER: (Scornfully, Sneeringly) Okay. But you said you thought that the book was *never* published!

GUEST: (Shrinking Away From Appraiser) I, I guess I don't really *know* whether it was ever published.

APPRAISER: (Pompously, Derisively) Actually the book *was* published!

GUEST: (Shaking now, edgy) Oh?

APPRAISER: (Patronizingly, Snootily) See? It says right at the bottom here, "Sketch for Noodle."

GUEST: (Tearfully, Nearly lying on the floor) Yes?

APPRAISER: (Uncaring, Heartless) Yes, see? It's signed right here. Noodle was a book that was written by Munro Leaf in 1937, and was a collaborative effort. Noodle the dachshund finds a wishbone and changes his appearance.

Certainly not a story that *I'd* ever read, but it is likely that this sketch, if it's *contemporaneous* with the book, would have been done in about 1936, a few years before the Madeline series and well before the 1961 Madeline in London.

GUEST: (Unable to speak, Whimpering)

Bemelmans have gone somewhat up in value considerably recently, considering how terrible they are. On this one, though, given that it *is* a full sketch, part of the estate, and a *fairly* interesting piece……..it's probably worth around…. $200,000 to $250,000!!!!

GUEST: (Hesitant, Sniffing) Wha..what did you say?

APPRAISER: (Amused, Entertained) And this one, Mr. Noodle, is, although not as famous, a wonderful sketch, and is worth probably around….$50,000!!

GUEST: (Uncertain, Still sniffing) Are you, are you kidding me? Really?

APPRAISER: (Unpleasantly, Spitefully) You did well,

congratulations. It's a really great pair.

GUEST: (Dizzy and sweaty from the stress of it all) Oh, I'm... I am astounded! That's, that's just great!

APPRAISER: (Hostile) Next!

House Hunters. That Costs *How* Much?!

Today's To-Do

- File Income Taxes Online - check
- Accidentally Clear Income Tax Return – check
- Give up and Look at 20yrs of Johnny Photos - check
- Another Cocktail – check
- Sex with Johnny..er, Hubby - check
- Clean up Dog poo on Living room rug – check
- Write Next Chapter for Best Selling Book - check
- Nap (maybe just a short one) – check

10:00p.m. Time to Buy a Home!

House Hunters #1

Biking Couple Searches for Eco-Friendly Home

Dillon and Cherry were excited to buy a home in the environmentally friendly and outdoorsy community of Boulder, Colorado. But sticker shock derailed them, right from the very start.

They quickly realized their $350,000 budget wouldn't go very far in pricey, trendy Boulder. So, they've decided to look instead at the slightly less pricey (and slightly less trendy) bedroom community of Louisville, for a three bedroom home with a big yard for their two huskies, Peace, and Harmony, and their two biodegradable bicycles, Sky and Willow.

The environmentally friendly couple hopes to have solar panels already installed, along with a designer compost bin. They also dream of someday building a wind powered greenhouse, where they can grow organic vegetables using only love as their fertilizer.

To complete their eco-lifestyle, they plan to bike to see the potential homes on their specially equipped bicycles, which capture and store the electricity generated during each ride. A ten mile trip alone will generate enough power to run a 4 watt light bulb for almost 3 full minutes!

Let's see what they find.

The first home is a four-bedroom tri-level, with a great floor plan and outdoor space. Cherry was concerned, however, about the lack of a built-in composter. This could really add to their initial costs!

Dillon also worried about the noxious chemicals that are *quite* likely being emitted from the new carpet. They'd need to pull that all out, to be replaced by more ecologically responsible sisal and hemp soul rugs.

The second home has loads of sunlight and a great layout, but it backs up to a busy street, where Dillon worries that the noxious chemicals spewing from the nasty oversized luxury cars, driven by nasty oversized luxury Republicans, might actually turn he and Cherry into religion crazed right-wing freaks.

Cherry worries that she may actually begin to *want* an oversized luxury car.

The third home has an open floor plan, but the back yard is extremely steep and they worry about their dog and whether they can have much of a garden.

Although the greenhouse *was* really nice, Dillon and Cherry feel that the cost to convert it to wind power might just be over their budget.

Final verdict!

We chose.........House #1!!

"The outdoor space was absolutely *perfect* for raising the chickens, and still leaves room to grow the oats for our homemade granola too!"

"Why, just from our profits on the eggs alone, we'll soon be able to finally custom design our 'dream composter!' We're SO excited, we just love it!!"

House Hunters#2

Biker Couple Searches for Kegger-Friendly Home

Slash and Sissy were excited to buy a home in the leathered and tattooed community of Frederick, Colorado. But sticker shock derailed them, right from the very start.

They quickly realized their $35,000 budget wouldn't go very far in this low-priced, low-brow Frederick. So, they've decided to look in the even lower-brow rural community of Erie, for a three bedroom trailer with a big yard for their bulldogs Spike and Fluffy, and their absurdly loud Harleys, Death-Wish and Ho-Throne.

The environmentally apathetic couple also hopes to have solar panels already installed, but mainly to power their new designer beer dispenser. And they too dream of someday building a gas powered greenhouse, but to grow some bitchin 'Mary Red Reefer' and 'Hard Hawaiian High', using only warm beer as their fertilizer.

To complete their eco-damaging lifestyle, they plan to bike to see the potential homes on their specially equipped Harleys, which capture and store the nasty fumes generated during each ride. A ten mile trip alone will generate more than enough fumes to take care of up to 3 rats at a time*! (* can vary, based on size and anger)

Let's see what they find.

The first home is a 1988 double-wide, with a floor plan and outdoor space (all 3x5 of it), not to mention a new chain-link fence around the front yard. Sissy was concerned, however, about the lack of a built-in beer dispenser (or at least a fridge in the garage). This could really add to their initial costs!

Slash also worried about the 10 foot Elm tree, growing in the middle of the driveway. They'd need to pull that out, to be replaced by more useful items like the 8 bikes and old cars that he's currently parting out on E-Bay.

The second home has loads of sunlight and a great metal awning over the back patio, but it backs up to a large wind-farm, where Slash worries that the bad vibes spewing from the outlandishly large windmills, promoted by the outlandishly green Democrats, might actually turn he and Sissy into socialist crazed left-wing freaks.

Sissy worries that she may actually begin to *want* an electric car.

The third home has an open floor plan, but the lack of plumbing, heating, and kitchen cabinets were a real turn-off. Although the greenhouse *was* really nice, Slash and Sissy feel that the cost to convert it to gas might just be too high.

Final verdict!

Editor's Note: Post-taping, Slash was very sadly laid off from his job as a Wal-Mart Greeter, while shortly afterward Sissy was switched from full-time to part-time coffee maker, at the Dunkin' Donut.

Due to these ill-fated events, they unfortunately no longer qualified for a mortgage.

Late Night (and other noise to have sex to)

Today's To-Do

- Clean Hubby's Drool from Sofa - check
- Turn out Lights – check
- Clean up Mess from Broken Lamp – check
- Apply Bandages to Cuts and Scratches - check
- Write Last Chapter for Best Selling Book - check
- Zzzzzzzzzzz

Time 11:00p.m .Time for Jay!

Fade In:

NBC Studios Jay Leno Show– Late Night (although, for some reason, it's taped at 8 o'clock in the morning)

(Lead in with big band rock music, giving special attention to the 'loud and blaring' saxophone player) (Cue applause)

                Jay

I'd like to thank you, Lori, for coming on the show and congratulations again on your 2012 World Book Award, for your latest bestseller!

I've read it three times, and just *couldn't* stop laughing! (Continue applause while Jay cracks up for 30 seconds)

But seriously, too, I also want to say, that we, *as a nation*, are so proud of your 'nearly single-handed victory' in finally getting rid of those nasty landmines! I've heard there's talk of a Nobel Prize! (Cue applause)

Lori

Well Jay, this is not about me and Johnny at all. It's really *all* about those *poor* people, and saving the *millions* of innocent lives! (Cue louder applause)

Jay

God you're beautiful!!!

Anyway, we certainly wish them (and you) the best! (Cue the loudest applause, along with a few loud 'Yeahs! and Whoohoos!')

Don't forget to look for Lori's soon to be out bestsellers, 'A Life Wasted..8 bits at a time (and other great things about the internet!)', also 'A Life Wasted..18 holes at a time (and other great things about golf)!' You can follow her blog 'A Life Wasted…A Thought at a Time (and other great things about life!)', at www.alifewastedbooks.com!

(Continue applause and loud 'Yeahs! and Whoohoos!', increase volume slowly)

Also, be sure to visit her interior design site, www.accent-the-positive.com for budget ideas on making your home look like a *million bucks*, for *under* $100! Remember that every time you click on an advertiser there, a $1 contribution goes to the 'Depp-Gee Landmine Fund'!!

Good night everybody!!!!

Fade out: (add the band back to the rest of the din) while Jay stares longingly into her Emerald Green eyes.

Epilogue

Finally

50,000 words (give or take)

Elapsed Time: Right around 46 minutes

Now it's time for the Wheel!

Look for these soon to be released titles:

A Life Wasted…1 Room at a Time (and other great things about home improvement!)

A Life Wasted…10 Pounds at a Time (and other great things about mid-life!)

A Life Wasted…8 Bits at a Time (and other great things about the internet!)

A Life Wasted…18 Holes at a Time (and other great things about golf!)

A Life Wasted…A Toy at a Time (and other great things about recreation!)

Also look for Lori's weekly blog:

A Life Wasted…A Thought at a Time (and other great things about life!)

www.alifewastedbooks.com

www.ingramcontent.com/pod-product-compliance
Lightning Source LLC
Chambersburg PA
CBHW071305040426
42444CB00009B/1877